Can we really HELP the Tigers?

Usborne

YES you can!

Katie Daynes
illustrated by Róisín Hahessy
designed by Helen Lee

The letter looks great!

Dear Purple Class,

Please come on a FREE VISIT to the zoo next Thursday. Bring pens and paper.

Yours most zookeeperly,

The Zookeeper

Will it fool the teacher?

Let's hope so!

We're PANGOLINS. Pangolins are so shy, no one really knows how many of us are left.

I've never heard of a PANGOLIN before. Are you a REPTILE?

No, we're MAMMALS – like you.

We give birth to little pangopups and feed them our milk.

YUM!

That's so cute. Why are YOU in danger?

Because people want to EAT us and make MEDICINES from our scales.

We curl into a ball to protect ourselves...

...but that just makes it EASIER for kidnappers to pick us up and carry us away!

HELP!

Kidnapping and killing endangered animals should be a CRIME.

It is!

It's called a WILDLIFE CRIME, and people can be arrested for it.

But the laws need to be stricter.

And governments need to take them more seriously.

Then we would be safe!

Hooray!

I bet no one would kidnap an elephant.

Maybe not, but they might try to hurt us.

I'm a monarch butterfly. We're struggling to find enough flowers to feed from...

...or the right leaves for our baby caterpillars to munch.

Stoneflies need crystal clear rivers for their young to grow up in...

ADULT FLY
YOUNG NYMPH
EGGS

...but most rivers are becoming too dirty.

Puffins are going hungry, because warmer seas mean fewer fish to eat.

RUMBLE RUMBLE

Aww, I LOVE puffins!

Sleepy dormice are losing their cosy hedgerow homes.

BBBRRRZZZ

And there are MANY more animals we could mention...

But **don't panic!**
It's not all doom and gloom.

Take BEAVERS for example.

In the past, they were hunted for their meat and fur until they nearly went EXTINCT.

Then humans realized they NEED beavers to keep rivers healthy.

Out you go.

Beavers build dams that slow the water down and clean it.

They create new habitats...

...and stop floods from happening further down the valley.

Now humans are HELPING beavers to recover in the wild – and the beavers are making things better for everyone.

27

Wow, go beavers! There must be things WE can do to help animals and nature recover...

YES!
You're more powerful than you might think.

Perhaps we could start by planting more flowers for the butterflies...

...and more trees to grow back the forests?

That would be BRILLIANT.

But how can we help YOU GUYS?

We can't stop people from chopping down trees,

kidnapping pangolins

or shooting tigers.

No, but you can tell others about how great we are...

...and the trouble we're in.

Ooh, if we tell the
PEOPLE IN POWER
all about you, they could make new
laws to PROTECT you.

Great idea.
You can explain how
protecting wild spaces
makes the world better for
EVERYONE.

Hmm. Humans might not be happy with that. But if you can find new ways to LINK UP our wild patches, then maybe humans and animals can SHARE the land.

Roads really get in the way.

How about we build animal crossings under them?

Or over them!

Excellent!

These are called wildlife corridors and they help all kinds of animals to survive.

I can't wait to tell my family everything I've learned today.

Pangolins, please can we make a poster about you to show our teacher?

Gosh, yes please.

Can you think of a cool fact to go on it?

Erm... that our tongues are as long as our bodies?

That's incredible!

How about you, little butterfly?

My jazzy pattern warns animals that I'm poisonous, so they don't eat me!

I never knew that!

What could I put on a poster about gorillas?

You could tell everyone that we're your distant cousins...

...so we're definitely worth protecting.

Oh wow, we're all part of the same family!

Anyone want a fun tiger fact?

Yes please!

No two tigers have the same stripes.

We're all unique!

Amazing.

A WEEK LATER, ON DISPLAY IN PURPLE CLASS...

What we all learned at the  ZOO

HELP THE TIGERS

Three sub-species of tiger have already DIED OUT.

How are tigers' stripes like fingerprints?

Each pattern is UNIQUE.

MONARCH BUTTERFLIES
have jazzy patterns to tell others they're POISONOUS!

ANIMALS ARE AMAZING. They'r

REWILD our world

STOP WILDLIFE CRIMES

WE ALL NEED WILD PLACES
Rain from rainforests waters our crops.
The wild makes us happy.
Trees help us breathe.

PROTECT THE PLANET FOR EVERYONE!

Elephant by Sasha

Sumatran tiger by Taz

Siberian tiger by Helen

ELEPHANTS
can walk **100 miles** in a day!

GORILLAS are our distant cousins.

PANGOLINS are mammals like us.

My tongue is as long as my body!

...lso **IN DANGER.** Let's spread the word and **HELP THEM.**

What do you think, Madam Mayor? I had no idea they'd learned so much at the zoo!

It's spectacular.

We should put it on display in the City Square.

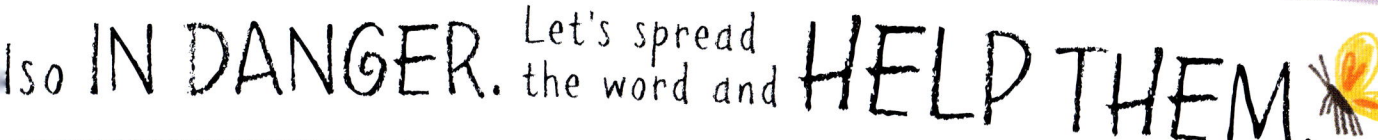

Gorilla by Mo

Our trip

What next?

The problems the animals describe in this book are REAL and affect us ALL. But the GOOD NEWS is that things are already changing...

Conservation groups have been working together to protect and enlarge tiger habitats. Since 2010, the number of tigers living in the wild has increased by 74%!

Today there are more than 6,000 national parks around the world. They're set up by governments to help protect wildlife.

WELCOME TO THE NATIONAL PARK

National parks in Kenya employ hundreds of local people as rangers. One of their main jobs is to stop anyone from hurting the elephants.

We used to try to make money by poaching elephants for their ivory tusks.

Now we're paid to protect them!

At one point there were only a few hundred Golden Lion Tamarins left in the wild. Now, there are several thousand.

A zoo rescued our grandparents.

Now we can live back in the wild!

Glossary

Here are some of the important words in this book and what they mean.

conference – a meeting organized to bring people (or animals!) together to talk about a chosen topic.

conservation – carefully preserving and protecting something. The characters in this book are particularly interested in nature conservation.

ecotourism – visiting places of natural beauty in a way that supports local people and respects nature.

extinct – no longer exists. An extinct species is one that has completely died out.

habitat – an animal or plant's natural home.

mammals – warm-blooded animals with a backbone that breathe air and feed milk to their young. Pangolins are the only mammals who are totally covered in scales.

national park – a natural area set aside by a government to preserve it and protect the plants and animals living there.

nature – all the animals, plants, and other things in the world that are not made by people.

oxygen – the gas we all need to breathe in to live.

poacher – a person who kills or takes wild animals illegally.

rainforest – a lush, dense forest that's rich in wildlife.

ranger – someone whose job is to protect a forest or natural park.

reptiles – cold-blooded animals with a backbone that breathe air and are covered in scales. Their young usually hatch out of soft-shelled eggs.

rewilding – restoring an area to its natural state.

species – a group of the same kind of living things. For example, the golden lion tamarin is a species of monkey.

vegan – not eating any foods that come from other animals.

wildlife corridor – a strip of land that connects two areas of habitat together.

wildlife crime – any activity that breaks the laws protecting animals and plants.

Usborne Quicklinks

For links to websites where you can meet tigers, elephants and other endangered animals, and find out more about how we can help protect them, go to usborne.com/Quicklinks and type in the title of this book.

Usborne Publishing is not responsible for the content of external websites. Children should be supervised online. Please follow the online safety guidelines at usborne.com/Quicklinks

Edited by Jane Chisholm
With expert advice from zoologist Dr. Tanesha Allen

First published in 2025 by Usborne Publishing Ltd., Usborne House, 83-85 Saffron Hill, London, EC1N 8RT. usborne.com Copyright © 2025 Usborne Publishing Ltd. The name Usborne and the balloon logo are trade marks of Usborne Publishing Ltd. All rights reserved. No part of this publication may be reproduced, stored in a retrieval system or transmitted in any form or by any means without the prior permission of the publisher. UE.

Usborne Publishing is not responsible for the availability or content of any website other than its own.